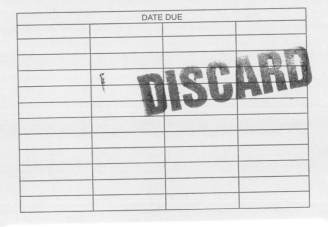

⟲⟲—THE GREAT OUTDOORS—⟳⟳

SALTWATER FISHING

Revised and Updated

by Laura Purdie Salas

Consultant:
Rich Novotny
Executive Director
Maryland Saltwater Sportfishermen's Association

Capstone
press®

Mankato, Minnesota

Edge Books are published by Capstone Press,
151 Good Counsel Drive, P.O. Box 669, Mankato, Minnesota 56002.
www.capstonepress.com

Salas, Laura Purdie.
    Saltwater fishing / by Laura Purdie Salas.—Rev. and updated.
    p. cm.—(Edge books. Great outdoors)
    Includes bibliographical references and index.
    ISBN-13: 978-1-4296-0824-4 (hardcover)
    ISBN-10: 1-4296-0824-2 (hardcover)
    1. Saltwater fishing—Juvenile literature. I. Title. II. Series.
SH457.S27 2008
799.16—dc22   2007011404

Summary: Describes the equipment, skills, conservation issues, and safety
concerns of saltwater fishing.

Editorial Credits
James Anderson, editor; Jo Miller, photo researcher; Tom Adamson, revised edition
    editor; Thomas Emery, revised edition designer; Kyle Grenz, revised edition
    production designer

Photo Credits
Ann and Rob Simpson, 15
Capstone Press/Gary Sundermeyer, 9, 19; Karon Dubke, cover
Corbis/Dale C. Spartas, 12, 33; Dan Lamont, 18; Joseph Sohm/ChromoSohm, Inc.,
    31; Mugshots, 26; Neil Rabinowitz, 5; Reuters NewMedia Inc., 37; Sygma, 35;
    Tom Stewart, 7; Tony Arruza, 29
Getty Images Inc./JPR, 11; Time Life Pictures, 20
photo courtesy of the Alaska Sealife Center, 44
Seapics.com/Doug Perrine, 40; Doug Stamm, 23, 45; Masa Uishoda 39, 41, 43;
    Richard Herrmann, 42; Walt Stearns, 25

1 2 3 4 5 6 12 11 10 09 08 07

TABLE OF CONTENTS

Features ━━━━━━━━━━━━━━━━━━━━━━━━━

Essential content terms are highlighted and are defined at the bottom of the page where they first appear.

Chapter 1

SALTWATER FISHING

Learn about the history of fishing, commercial fishing, and sport fish.

Saltwater fishing is a popular activity around the world. People who saltwater fish are called anglers. North American anglers fish in the Atlantic and Pacific Oceans or the Gulf of Mexico. They fish from boats, piers, and the shore.

People have been catching fish for thousands of years. Anglers once tied a line around a sharp piece of bone, wood, or shell. They put the sharp piece inside bait, such as a small fish. The anglers pulled the line tight when a larger fish swallowed the bait. The sharp piece caught in the fish's mouth.

Saltwater fishing is a popular sport.

The United States' first president was a saltwater angler. In 1790, newspaper reporters wrote about President George Washington's fishing trips. Washington fished for sea bass and blackfish.

President George H. W. Bush fished near his family's land in Maine. He fished for bluefish for 18 days in 1989.

Bodyguards crowded around him in their own boats and may have scared the fish away. Bush fished for 17 days without a bite. He finally caught a 10-pound (4.5-kilogram) bluefish on the last day of his vacation.

Saltwater Fishing Today

People who fish for fun are called recreational anglers. More than 15 million people saltwater fish for fun in the United States. In 2002, these anglers caught about 440 million fish. About 380,000 anglers fish in waters off Canada. They catch more than 7 million fish each year.

EDGE FACT —⟨◉⟩

On average, each American consumed 3.1 pounds (1.4 kilograms) of tuna in 2005.

Commercial fishers catch fish to sell.

Saltwater fishing is an important industry in North America. People who sell their catch for money are called commercial fishers. They sell fish to supermarkets and restaurants. Commercial fishers caught almost 100 times as many fish as recreational anglers did in 2002.

Modern equipment helps make saltwater fishing easier for many people. Stronger rods and lines allow anglers to catch bigger fish. Depth finders help anglers locate areas where fish might be. Faster boats let anglers cover large areas.

Types of Fish

Anglers around the world catch more than 700 types of saltwater fish. Many people fish in the oceans for sport fish. Sport fish include marlin, sailfish, and sharks. These fish are not caught for food but for the thrill and challenge of the catch.

Most fish caught in salt water can be eaten. Some anglers focus on catching halibut, cod, and tuna.

EDGE FACT

The world record marlin catch is held by A.C. Glassell Jr. On August 4, 1953, he caught a black marlin that weighed 1,560 pounds (708 kilograms) off the coast of Peru.

Tuna Teriyaki
Serves: 4   *Children should have adult supervision.*

Ingredients:
4 tuna steaks
⅓ cup (80 mL) soy sauce
1 tablespoon (15 mL) honey
1 tablespoon (15 mL) chopped ginger
1 teaspoon (5 mL) minced garlic
2 tablespoons (30 mL) vegetable oil

Equipment:
9-inch by 13-inch (23-centimeter by 33-centimeter) glass baking dish
cooking spray
medium bowl
metal spatula
mixing spoon
pastry brush

What You Do:
1. Lightly coat baking dish with cooking spray.
2. Place steaks in baking dish.
3. In bowl, make marinade by mixing soy sauce, honey, ginger, garlic, and vegetable oil.
4. Pour the marinade over the tuna steaks.
5. Place in refrigerator to marinate for 30 minutes.
6. Use pastry brush to brush tops of steaks with marinade.
7. Broil or grill for 4 minutes, about 4 to 6 inches (10 to 15 centimeters) from heat source.
8. Turn steaks over with metal spatula. Brush marinade over steaks.
9. Broil or grill for 4 more minutes.

Chapter 2

EQUIPMENT

Learn about fishing rods, boats, bait, and more.

Basic saltwater fishing equipment includes rods and reels, line, bait, and lures. Serious anglers might use electronic items and a variety of tools.

Rods and Reels

Saltwater anglers use fishing rods made from graphite or fiberglass. These rods bend easily. Saltwater fishing rods are between 5 and 12 feet (2 and 4 meters) long.

Rods have a reel attached to them. Reels hold the fishing line. Reels allow anglers to cast and collect the line. Anglers turn a crank on the reel to pull in the line.

Most saltwater fishing equipment is larger than gear used for freshwater fishing.

Lines

Anglers use fishing line that is strong enough for the fish they are trying to catch. They must keep a good hold on the line to keep the fish hooked. But too much tension can break the line. Most reels have a drag system, which allows the line to be pulled off before breaking.

Bringing in a Fish

The angler must make a decision once the fish is close to the boat. Some anglers don't want to keep the fish they catch. They release the fish without lifting it into the boat.

Anglers use leaders, nets, or gaffs to bring the fish into the boat. A gaff is a large metal hook. Anglers stick their catch with the hook and pull up the fish.

A leader is a piece of strong wire that attaches the fishing line to the hook. It is much stronger than the fishing line that is on the reel. A leader can handle the weight of heavy fish.

Bait

Saltwater anglers use many types of live bait. Small fish are the most popular bait. The size of the bait depends on the size of the fish an angler is trying to catch. An angler might use a 2-pound (1-kilogram) mullet to catch a 15-pound (7-kilogram) tuna. Large chunks of tuna might be used to catch a 500-pound (227-kilogram) tiger shark. Other live bait includes shrimp, crabs, worms, and shellfish.

gaff—a hook used for bringing in a fish

Anglers use natural bait to make chum. Anglers place cut-up fish in a net bag and drag it behind the boat. The blood and oil from the fish create a smelly trail in the water for other fish to follow. Mackerel, snapper, butterfish, and tuna are a few fish that anglers attract with chum.

Lures

Anglers also use lures. These artificial objects attract fish. Lures are made of feathers, metal, plastic, wood, yarn, and other materials.

Some lures look like a fish's natural food. Flies are lures that look like insects. People make flies from feathers or animal hair. Imitations are plastic lures that look like frogs, earthworms, or small fish. Plugs are wooden lures that look like small fish.

Clothing

Anglers protect themselves from sun, wind, and water. Hats protect their face and head from sunburn.

artificial—made by people

14

Waterproof jackets and pants keep anglers dry and warm. Waterproof boots or shoes are helpful because the bottom of the boat tends to gets wet. Surf fishers who wade into water also need waterproof boots.

Most anglers wear jackets and vests with lots of pockets. Anglers store lures and other items in the pockets. Jackets and shirts must be loose around the shoulders and arms. Loose-fitting clothing allows the angler to cast easily.

Boats

Anglers use many kinds of fishing boats. Some anglers rent a spot on a party boat. Party boats depart on a regular schedule and can stay out all day. A spot on a party boat can cost from $30 to more than $100. Some party boats have tackle for anglers to use or rent. Some party boats hold more than 100 anglers.

One angler or a small group of anglers can rent a charter boat. A guide from the charter company runs the boat and gives advice about fishing. A charter boat costs $300 or more per person. A party of five or six people might rent a charter boat for a day.

Some anglers use small utility boats. Utility boats are 12 to 18 feet (4 to 5 meters) long. Utility boats are best for calm water.

Anglers who travel on rough water use cruisers. These boats range from 18 to 40 feet (5 to 12 meters) long. Cruisers travel faster than utility boats. Cruisers can be used for overnight trips. They have areas below the deck called berths. People can sleep in berths.

Some saltwater anglers do not use a boat. They fish from shore. Fishing from shore is called surf fishing. Other anglers fish from piers and bridges.

Other Gear

Saltwater fishers need several other items for a successful fishing trip.

- **Sinkers**—small metal weights that hold the bait deep in the water
- **Bobbers**—devices that float on the surface and keep bait from sinking too far
- **Depth Finder**—electronic device that uses sound waves to find objects underwater; depth finders have a screen where anglers can see images of the ocean floor
- **Contour Maps**—show the formation of the ocean's floor
- **Nautical Charts**—for navigation; these charts show the coastline and the depth of the water; they also show tides, lighthouses, and other items to help anglers find their way on the ocean
- **Global Positioning System (GPS)**—uses satellites in space to find a fisher's favorite fishing spots and to navigate safely

nautical—having to do with navigating at sea

Saltwater Fishing—Equipment

Legend

1. Jacket
2. Sunglasses
3. PFD (Personal Flotation Device)
4. Bait Pail
5. Depth Finder
6. Fishing Rod
7. Fishing Line
8. Net
9. Filet Knife
10. Lure
11. Pliers

Crab fishers hoist a heavy crab pot out of the sea.

EDGE FACT ⟶

The injury rate for crab fishing is nearly 100 percent.

Alaska king crab is a popular seafood worldwide. However, crab fishing is one of the most dangerous jobs in the world. King crab are harvested in the Bering Sea in October and January. The weather there is terrible at those times. The rough sea tosses the boats around, and the fishers are pounded by the icy wind, rain, and waves.

Fishers have to hoist 700-pound (318-kilogram) tanks, called crab pots, into the sea. The pots and other dangerous equipment can cause broken fingers, ribs, and legs. It's not unusual for fishers to get thrown overboard into the frigid water during times of rough seas. Besides the danger, they work about 20 hours a day.

So why bother? Crab fishers can earn as much as $50,000 in just those two months of strenuous work.

Chapter 3

SKILLS AND TECHNIQUES

Learn about fishing locations, the best times to fish, and fishing techniques.

Saltwater anglers build up knowledge and experience to make good decisions. They learn about the best places to fish. They find out what time of day fish are most active. They also must know how to choose bait and fishing methods.

Locations

Knowing about fish habitats can help anglers decide where to fish. Fish prefer certain areas to feed and swim. Anglers need to know the usual location of the fish they want to catch.

habitat—the natural place and conditions in which fish live

An angler chooses the right bait and location to catch a barracuda.

Some fish like to feed near strong currents. Large fish eat small fish and shrimp that the currents carry. Many anglers like to fish when the tide is coming in or going out. When the tide shifts, fish look for food in the currents.

Some fish like to swim in warm water. These fish include sailfish, marlin, and tiger sharks. Shallow water is often warmer than deep water.

Other types of fish live in colder water. Cod and Atlantic mackerel live in cold water.

Most fish hide in cover. Cover might be a wrecked ship, coral reefs, or the space between the posts that hold up a pier. Groupers and snapper swim near coral reefs.

When to Fish

Saltwater anglers choose their fishing time based on what kind of fish they want to catch. Fish are more active during feeding periods. Snook feed day and night, but sharks feed more at night. Anglers learn the active times for different fish species.

Anglers also choose their fishing time based on their fishing spot. Nighttime is best for pier fishing. Bait fish are attracted to the lights around the pier. Anglers catch the bigger fish that come to feed on the bait fish.

Surf fishers do their fishing during early morning and evening hours.

Saltwater Fishing—Methods

Fishing Methods

There are many ways to saltwater fish. Some common methods are surf fishing, still fishing, drift fishing, chumming or chunking, trolling, and jigging.

Surf fishers catch the most fish in the early morning or late evening. During the day, sandy beaches offer no cover. During the early morning and late evening, the sun casts more shadows. Fish use shadowy water as cover.

The still fishing method can be used from a pier or an anchored boat. The angler lets the bait stay in the water. Drift fishers also let their bait stay in the water. But they let their boat drift with the current. Still and drift fishers catch giant sea bass, rockfish, and barracuda.

Anglers can anchor their boat for chumming or chunking. Chum is cut-up or ground-up bait fish. Fishers place the chum in a net bag and toss it into the water to attract fish. Chunking is similar. The bait fish are cut into much larger chunks.

An angler uses a moving boat to troll. The angler lets the line trail behind the boat. Anglers can also troll while walking on a bridge or pier. They let the line trail as they walk. Trolling is a good way to catch groupers, bluefish, tuna, and marlin.

Anglers in an anchored boat or on a pier or bridge can jig. Anglers who jig let the lure fall down and then jerk it up again. They keep the lure moving constantly.

Fish that are attracted to movement might strike a jig. These fish include grunts, black sea bass, and some kinds of tuna. The fish may leap out of the water when they go after a jigging lure.

Saltwater Fishing—Methods

While trolling, anglers let their line trail behind a moving boat.

Chapter 4

CONSERVATION

Learn about limits, catch-and-release methods, and pollution.

Responsible anglers protect fish and their habitats. The sport of saltwater fishing depends on clean water and healthy fish.

Licenses and Regulations

Government groups set rules for anglers. Anglers buy a license. License sales tell the government how many people go fishing and where they like to fish.

Laws set limits on the number of fish an angler can take home each day. Different types of fish have different limits. Limits make sure that there will be fish left for other anglers.

Government groups also decide minimum sizes of fish that can be caught. Anglers must release fish that are too small. These rules help fish survive long enough to reproduce.

Polluted beaches must be cleaned before anglers can fish from the water.

Releasing Fish

Anglers release fish they do not want to keep. They put the fish back into the water. They also release fish that are not legal to keep. This form of fishing is called catch-and-release.

Anglers handle fish gently to avoid injuring the fish. Anglers try to remove the hook while the fish is in water. A fish out of water cannot breathe. A fish will die if it spends too much time out of the water.

Protecting Water Sources

Responsible anglers keep water clean. Polluted water enters fish's bodies and can make fish sick. It can even kill fish. Waste from farming, industry, and cars pollute the ocean.

Anglers can help conservation efforts by acting responsibly. They should leave the ocean as clean as or cleaner than they found it. They should not throw litter into the ocean.

An angler releases a bonefish.

Oil Spills

Oil spills are a major water pollutant. Large ships carrying oil have crashed and spilled oil into the oceans. The oil has damaged fish habitats. Many sea animals such as birds, sea otters, and whales have also been destroyed by oil spills.

The *Exxon Valdez* caused the largest oil spill in recent history. On March 24, 1989, the tanker became stuck on Bligh Reef off the coast of Alaska. The ship spilled 11 million gallons (42 million liters) of oil into the Pacific Ocean.

The oil killed millions of fish and other animals. The fishing industry was hurt by the spill. Many fishing companies had to find other places to fish.

EDGE FACT —⊙⌒☉⁾

The cost of cleaning up the Exxon Valdez *oil spill was at least $2 billion.*

People work together to clean beaches and water after an oil spill.

Chapter 5

SAFETY

Learn about weather safety, sun protection, and handling dangerous equipment.

Saltwater fishing can be dangerous. Bad weather can threaten fishing boats on the ocean. Anglers should always wear personal flotation devices while in the boat. They should know the weather reports. Anglers should always fish with a partner, and they should have rescue skills.

Weather

Anglers check the weather forecast before leaving shore. They stay on land if storms are predicted. They also check wave height. Many anglers do not go on the water if waves are taller than 3 feet (1 meter).

Anglers watch for lightning. Lightning often strikes the highest target. Anglers take down fishing rods and stay as low in the boat as possible. They move to shore quickly.

Hurricanes and other storms can cause great damage to boats.

Dressing Safely

Storms are not the only weather dangers. Anglers need to protect themselves from sunburn. They wear sunscreen on any uncovered skin. They also wear hats and sunglasses.

Anglers need warm, dry clothes. Anglers usually have an extra set of dry clothes. They should wear a waterproof outer layer of clothing. Anglers should be prepared for changing weather conditions.

Equipment Safety

Saltwater anglers handle dangerous objects. Fish hooks, knives, and gaffs should always be placed where people will not cut themselves.

Safety is a big concern for many anglers. Safe anglers make saltwater fishing an enjoyable sport for everyone.

Anglers use hats or visors and sunglasses to protect them from the sun's rays.

Bluefish

Description: Bluefish are blue along the top and silver along the sides. They have two dorsal fins. Bluefish have sharp teeth. They weigh 3 to 15 pounds (1 to 7 kilograms).

Habitat: near the surface, around coastal areas and structures

Food: smaller fish

Bait and lures: menhaden, herring, chum, flies, jigs

Black Grouper

Description: Black groupers have olive or gray bodies with black spots. They weigh around 10 pounds (5 kilograms). Groupers are powerful for their size.

Habitat: offshore reefs, shipwrecks, ridges, ocean bottom

Food: smaller fish

Bait and lures: pinfish, grunts, goggleyes, leadhead jigs

Bluefin Tuna

Description: The bluefin tuna's blue color fades to silver on its side and belly. These slim fish can grow to almost 1,500 pounds (680 kilograms).

Habitat: deep water, but they come close to the surface to feed

Food: mackerel, herring, squid, bluefish

Bait and lures: mackerel, skipjack, spoons, jigs, plastic squid

Blue Marlin

Description: Blue marlin are bright blue on top, fading to silver on the sides and belly. Some grow as heavy as 1,500 pounds (680 kilograms).

Habitat: deep waters, warm offshore water, weedy areas

Food: bonito, tuna, dolphin

Bait and lures: trolling with mackerel, bonito, lures that dive and bubble

Pacific Halibut

Description: Pacific halibut are dark on one side. Both eyes are on this side. Its other side is light. Halibut swim with the light side facing the ocean floor. Some pacific halibut can grow as large as 450 pounds (204 kilograms).

Habitat: deep, cold water; areas with flat bottoms of mud, sand, or gravel; areas with strong currents

Food: herring, smaller fish

Bait and lures: herring with heavy tackle, heavy jigs, sinking flies

Striped Bass

Description: Striped bass are called stripers. Stripers are silver. They have seven or eight stripes along each side. They weigh 5 to 10 pounds (2 to 5 kilograms). They can grow as large as 75 pounds (34 kilograms).

Habitat: in bays and close to shore in both salt and freshwater

Food: herring

Bait and lures: squid, herring, crabs, jigs, flies

GLOSSARY

charter (CHAR-tur)—relating to a travel arrangement in which a boat is hired for a group of people to use

chum (CHUHM)—chopped fish that is used as bait

commercial (kuh-MUR-shuhl)—to do with buying and selling things

habitat (HAB-uh-tat)—the natural place and conditions in which animals live

nautical (NAW-tuh-kuhl)—to do with navigating at sea

pier (PIHR)—a platform that extends over a body of water

pollutant (puh-LOOT-uhnt)—a harmful material that can damage the environment

species (SPEE-sheez)—a group of animals with similar features

READ MORE

Bryan, Nichol. *Exxon Valdez Oil Spill.* Environmental Disasters. Milwaukee: World Almanac Library, 2004.

Hopkins, Ellen. *Freshwater Fishing.* Rev. Ed. The Great Outdoors. Mankato, Minn.: Capstone Press, 2008.

Wessman, Bo. *Complete Guide to Fishing: Building Your Own Rod.* Broomall, Penn.: Mason Crest, 2004.

INTERNET SITES

FactHound offers a safe, fun way to find Internet sites related to this book. All of the sites on FactHound have been researched by our staff.

Here's how:

1. Visit *www.facthound.com*

2. Choose your grade level.

3. Type in this book ID **1429608242** for age-appropriate sites. You may also browse subjects by clicking on letters, or by clicking pictures and words.

4. Click on the **Fetch It** button.

FactHound will fetch the best sites for you!

INDEX